No Horn Unicorn

Written by Shani Dhanda

Illustrated by Letizia Rizzo

Collins

Chapter 1

Somewhere between the Quiet Mountains and a bright blue waterfall lies Wildberry Forest. Here, birds sing their songs and fairies dance in and out of the trees. Fairies work and play, spreading joy everywhere, while rabbits hop and squirrels scurry. Butterflies flutter in bright colours, and deer peacefully munch on the grass. It's such a beautiful place to live.

Ugo

Uni

Una

Wildberry Forest is also home to Ugo the unicorn, just one of the unique and special animals living with a herd of other unicorns. Ugo's closest friends are Uni, Una, Ulix and Ushi. Together they explore enchanted meadows, chase shimmering rainbows, and go on adventures.

Ugo looks a bit different from other unicorns because he doesn't have a horn. Sometimes his friends aren't very kind about it.

Ulix

Ushi

Chapter 2

At a gathering near the bright blue waterfall, all the unicorns were using their long, white, glowing horns to create a beautiful rainbow.

Ugo tried to create a rainbow, just like the other unicorns, by leaning his head into the waterfall.

"You can't do it like *that!*" Ulix smirked.

"You can't make rainbows without a horn," Uni said.

I have made a rainbow, Ugo thought. *It's just a different kind of rainbow.*

When it was time to gather berries from the tall bushes, all the unicorns were using their horns to reach them.

Ugo approached the bushes with excitement. He loved juicy berries.

Ugo tried to get the berries, like his friends. He rustled the branches with his hooves, but the other unicorns shook their heads.

"You can't do it like *that*!" Una said.

"Without a horn, you can't reach the berries!" Ushi said.

Ugo slowly trotted away from the bushes. He was
hoping one of the others might call him back,
but no one did. *There are lots of ways to get berries,*
Ugo thought. *I just do it differently.*

Chapter 3

The next day was the fairies' annual hide-and-seek competition in Wildberry Forest, and Ugo was excited to join in the fun.

I'm really good at hiding, Ugo thought. *Maybe the other unicorns will remember that and be kinder today.*

Hide-and-seek competition

As the game began, Uni, Una, Ulix and Ushi scurried to find the best hiding spots. But the unicorns were finding it a bit difficult to hide because of their long horns.

Ugo didn't have any difficulty. Without a horn,
he skilfully used his natural colours to blend with
the greenery. Weaving through the trees with grace,
Ugo's unique appearance helped him disappear into
the forest.

Uni, Una, Ulix and Ushi were soon found by the fairies. They searched high and low for Ugo, but he'd vanished.

"Where could Ugo be?" Ulix wondered.

Little did they know that Ugo was right in front of them, cleverly hidden in the green leaves and branches.

Chapter 4

The day grew longer, and still nobody had found Ugo. The fairies' annual hide-and-seek competition had never gone on this long before.

Uni called out, "Ugo, you can't hide forever!"

But Ugo was having great fun, hiding among the forest greenery, and changing his hiding place as it was getting darker.

Ugo was determined to win the competition. The clever unicorn wanted to prove to his friends that just because he was born without a horn, it didn't mean he couldn't do things or be good at things. Ugo was going to stay hidden for as long as possible, then jump out when the other unicorns weren't expecting it!

Night fell and Uni, Una, Ulix and Ushi were really worried about Ugo. They hadn't seen him since they were unkind the day before, and they missed their friend. They also felt guilty.

"We need to search for Ugo together," Una said.

"When we find Ugo, we can make things right," Ushi replied.

Uni nodded. "I'm sorry for what we said."

Off they went, searching high and low in the forest, shouting, "Ugo, Ugo!"

"Do you remember how kind Ugo was when he helped to decorate the fairy houses with flowers?" Uni said. "He's so creative."

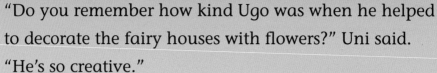

"And wasn't Ugo funny when he ate a dandelion and ended up with a fluffy yellow beard?" Ulix said.

Una nodded. "I'll never forget when Ugo showed us how to build a secret hideout in the ancient tree. It became our special place for storytelling and dreams."

Ushi added, "Remember when he organised the forest concert? Ugo brought everyone together in Wildberry Forest. It was the best night."

Chapter 5

They called out Ugo's name for what felt like hours.

"Let's stop for a rest," Ulix said, as they reached the tall berry bushes.

"This is where we last saw Ugo yesterday," Uni remembered.

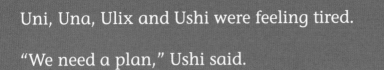

Uni, Una, Ulix and Ushi were feeling tired.

"We need a plan," Ushi said.

"Let's ask our other forest friends to help us search for Ugo," Una suggested.

Suddenly, there was a rustling nearby.

The unicorns stopped talking for a moment.
They heard a strange sound in the air, which sent
shivers down the spines of Ugo's unicorn friends.
Their eyes widened with alarm.

Ulix, with trembling hooves, whispered,
"What was that?"

Uni decided to be brave and took the lead.
She was determined to discover the source of
the mysterious sound. "Follow me!" she whispered.

With a careful trot, Uni followed the faint noise deeper
into the forest. The others trotted behind her. As they
approached a cluster of tall berry bushes, the sound
got louder and louder. Una, Ulix and Ushi nudged
Uni forward.

"It sounds like Ugo," Uni said. "I think he's in trouble!"

Ugo *was* in trouble! While he was waiting to jump out on the others, one of his legs had got caught in a crack in the rocks.

"Ushi, Una. You pull Ugo from the back," Uni said. "Ulix and I will push from the front!"

They pushed and they pulled until Ugo was free!

"Oh, thank you!" Ugo said. "I've been hiding for hours, and I was so hungry I didn't see where I was stepping."

"We're so glad we found you!" Uni said.

"We're sorry for what we said earlier," Una said.

"We shouldn't have treated you differently just because you don't have a horn," Ushi added.

Uni nodded. "You're great just the way you are."

"*And* you're the best player at hide-and-seek," said Ulix. "We can't do that!"

"I find it really easy; I just don't like all the waiting to be found," chuckled Ugo. "Let's go home!"

Ugo forgave the other unicorns, and the warmth of their friendship filled his heart.

They learned that being themselves made their friendship even better. It didn't matter if they had horns or not; what counted was accepting each other for who they were. True friends accept you for you, and that's what makes friendship so magical.

The tale of Ugo, the unicorn without a horn, became a legend. The forest echoed with laughter and joy as the unicorns, with and without horns, played together.

Ugo tried to teach the others how to hide, but they were never quite as good as him.

I can do that!

I can create beautiful rainbows.

I can make beautiful decorations.

I can build good camps.

30

I can make
others laugh.

I can organise
a concert.

I can help my friends.

Ideas for reading

Written by Christine Whitney
Primary Literacy Consultant

Reading objectives:
- make inferences on the basis of what is being said and done
- answer and ask questions
- predict what might happen on the basis of what has been read so far
- discuss and clarify the meanings of words
- discuss the sequence of events in books and how items of information are related

Spoken language objectives:
- participate in discussions
- use spoken language to develop understanding through speculating, hypothesising, imagining and exploring ideas
- ask relevant questions

Curriculum links: PSHE Education: learn about what is kind and unkind behaviour, and how this can affect others; learn to recognise the ways in which they are the same and different to others; learn how to listen to other people and play and work cooperatively

Interest words: unicorn, enchanted, legend

Word count: 1221

Build a context for reading
- Before looking at the book, encourage children to share their knowledge of unicorns. What is unique about them? What stories have they read about unicorns?
- Look at the title on the front cover, then closely at the illustration. Discuss where this story might be set.
- Read the blurb on the back cover. Ask children to suggest what problems Ugo might face.

Understand and apply reading strategies
- Read Chapter 1 together. Ask children to find words and phrases that show this is a fantasy story.
- Continue to read together up to the end of Chapter 2. Ask children to summarise the relationship between Ugo and the other unicorns.